JOHN WESLEY POWELL
AND THE ANTHROPOLOGY OF
THE CANYON COUNTRY

John Wesley Powell and Southern Paiute Indians. Photograph by J. K. Hillers, 1873, from Smithsonian Institution, Bureau of American Ethnology Collection.

John Wesley Powell and the Anthropology of the Canyon Country

By DON D. FOWLER, ROBERT C. EULER, *and* CATHERINE S. FOWLER

GEOLOGICAL SURVEY PROFESSIONAL PAPER 670

A description of John Wesley Powell's anthropological fieldwork, the archeology of the Canyon Country, and extracts from Powell's notes on the origins, customs, practices, and beliefs of the Indians of that area

UNITED STATES GOVERNMENT PRINTING OFFICE, WASHINGTON: 1969
reprinted by Grand Canyon Natural History Association: 1977, 1981

UNITED STATES DEPARTMENT OF THE INTERIOR

WALTER J. HICKEL, *Secretary*

GEOLOGICAL SURVEY

William T. Pecora, *Director*

Library of Congress catalog-card No. 77–601670

Contents

	Page
Abstract	1
Introduction	1
John Wesley Powell's anthropological fieldwork, by Don D. Fowler and Catherine S. Fowler	2
The archeology of the Canyon Country, by Robert C. Euler	8
The ethnography of the Canyon Country, by Don D. Fowler and Catherine S. Fowler	20
Extracts from John Wesley Powell's notes on the Indians	22
Means of subsistence	22

	Page
Extracts from John Wesley Powell's notes on the Indians—Continued	
Animal food	25
Courtship and marriage	26
Mythology and beliefs	27
The boundaries of the earth	27
The origin of the cañons of the Colorado	27
The origin of mountains, valleys, [and] cañons	28
Origin of the Pai-Utes	28
References cited	28

Illustrations

FRONTISPIECE. John Wesley Powell and Southern Paiute Indians.

		Page
FIGURES 1–6.	Photographs showing:	
	1. Kaibab Paiute Indians	3
	2. Powell meeting with Kaibab Paiutes	4
	3. The Powell-Ingalls Special Commission meeting with Southern Paiutes	5
	4. Naches, one of Powell's Northern Paiute informants	6
	5. Southern Paiute women wearing Ute dresses	6
	6. Powell with Ute woman and a posed group of Kaibab Paiute men	7
7.	Map showing distribution of the archeological cultures of the Canyon Country and Great Basin	9
8.	Photograph showing ruin on ledge near mouth of White Canyon, Utah	10
9.	Map showing eastern part of Grand Canyon, Ariz	11
10–14.	Photographs showing:	
	10. Kayenta Anasazi masonry structure opposite Unkar Creek	12
	11. Ruins at the mouth of Bright Angel Creek	13
	12. Ruins at the confluence of Crystal Creek and the Colorado River	14
	13. Ruins above mouth of Shinumo Canyon	16
	14. Ruins along Tapeats Creek	19
15.	Map showing distribution of historic tribes of the Canyon Country and Great Basin	20
16–18.	Photographs showing:	
	16. Tapeats, one of Powell's Southern Paiute informants	21
	17. Kaibab Paiute camp on Kaibab Plateau	22
	18. Kaibab Paiute woman working with metate and mano, grinding seeds into meal	24

JOHN WESLEY POWELL AND THE ANTHROPOLOGY OF THE CANYON COUNTRY

By Don D. Fowler,[1] Robert C. Euler,[2] and Catherine S. Fowler[3]

Abstract

From 1868 to 1879, John Wesley Powell devoted part of his time to a study of the Indians of the Canyon Country—those areas of Utah, western Colorado, northern Arizona, and northwestern New Mexico that are drained by the Colorado River and its tributaries. In 1879, Congress provided money for the completion of Powell's ethnological work, and this led to the creation of the Smithsonian Institution's Bureau of American Ethnology. More than 250 archeological sites have been found below the rims of Marble and Grand Canyons; 37 of the sites are along Powell's river route, but only eight are recorded in Powell's reports or in the journals of those who went with him. The prehistoric human history of the Grand Canyon region is briefly described here by R. C. Euler. The origins of the Indians in the Canyon Country are portrayed by D. D. and C. S. Fowler, and brief accounts are presented, using quotations from Powell's notes, on Indian customs, practices, and beliefs.

INTRODUCTION

On May 24, 1869, John Wesley Powell and nine volunteers started down the Green River from Green River Station, Wyoming Territory. Their aim was to map and to collect scientific information about the Canyon Country—those areas of Utah, western Colorado, northern Arizona, and northwestern New Mexico drained by the Colorado River and its tributaries. Powell and his men completed the trip on August 30, 1869, when they arrived at the mouth of the Virgin River below the Grand Canyon. Powell and other volunteers made a second trip in 1871–72 but concluded their exploration at the mouth of Kanab Creek in the Grand Canyon. The story of these trips is well known and will not be repeated here.[4]

Powell's exploits made him a national hero. After his 1869 trip, Powell sought and received a congressional appropriation to continue his research. The appropriation, continued in later years, established the Geographical and Geological Survey of the Rocky Mountain Region, J. W. Powell in Charge. Powell's Rocky Mountain Survey became the fourth of the so-called great surveys (Bartlett, 1962) operating in the American West after the Civil War. The others operated under F. V. Hayden, Clarence King, and Lt. G. W. Wheeler.

Throughout the 1870's, Powell and the men who worked under him carried out extensive geological and topographic studies in the Canyon Country. Some of these studies remain as classics in the field, especially Powell's (1875a, 1876) on the canyons of the Colorado and the Uinta Mountains, G. K. Gilbert's (1877) on the Henry Mountains, and C. E. Dutton's (1880) on the Grand Canyon.

This paper is concerned with yet another facet of Powell's work in the Canyon Country—his studies of the archeological remains and of the historic Indian tribes of the region.

Research by D. D. Fowler on the materials in the introductory and ethnography sections of this paper were made possible by a National Research Council postdoctoral visiting research associateship at the Smithsonian Institution in 1967–68 and by a grant from the National Endowment for the Humanities. This support is gratefully acknowledged. R. C. Euler wishes to express his appreciation to the Arizona Power Authority, the National Park Service, Dr. and Mrs. F. E. Bumgarner, and the National Science Foundation (Grant GS–1078) for financial support of his Grand Canyon research, of which this study is a part. To the late Rod Sanderson and his sons, of Page, Ariz., who expertly piloted him on

---

[1] Desert Research Institute, University of Nevada, Reno, Nev.
[2] Prescott College, Prescott, Ariz.
[3] University of Nevada, Reno, Nev.
[4] See Darrah (1951) and Stegner (1954). Several diaries and journals of both trips were kept. See Gregory (1939), Darrah, Chamberlin, and Kelly (1947), Darrah, Gregory, and Kelly (1948–49), Dellenbaugh (1908), Fowler and Fowler (1969a). Powell's own published narratives (1875a, 1895) telescope the events of both trips and report them as taking place in 1869.

four Colorado River trips through Grand Canyon, and to Wayne Learn, the skilled helicopter pilot with whom he has spent so many hours flying the tortuous byways of the canyon, his everlasting gratitude for those always exciting yet always safe journeys. Finally, a note of thanks to his wife, Elizabeth, for smoothing the archeology section with her editorial comments.

JOHN WESLEY POWELL'S ANTHROPOLOGICAL FIELDWORK

By Don D. Fowler and Catherine S. Fowler

Powell's first acquaintance with the Indians of the Canyon Country came in 1868. He was then leading his second expedition of volunteer students and friends on a natural history expedition into the Rocky Mountains. In the fall, the party journeyed to the White River in northwestern Colorado. Most of them turned northward and returned home via the railroad at Green River Station, Wyo., but Powell, his wife Emma, and three men remained on the White River for the winter.

Powell's purpose was to determine the feasibility of a boat expedition down the then largely unknown Green and Colorado Rivers, and he spent much of the winter making reconnaissance trips along the rims of the Green River and its tributaries.

He did not devote all of the winter of 1868–69 to geology and reconnaissance, however. A band of Tabuats Ute Indians, led by Chief Douglass, was also camped on the White River near Powell's camp. Powell spent many long winter evenings learning the language and observing the customs of the Indians. His knowledge of the Ute-Southern Paiute language, which he continued to study in later years, served him well during his work in the Canyon Country. The Utes dubbed him Kapurats, meaning "arm off," a name still remembered by some of the Indians of southern Utah and northern Arizona. In 1967, an old Kaibab Paiute woman from northern Arizona told one of the authors that Kapurats was remembered by her people as the man who many years ago tied rags on trees (apparently referring to the surveying tape used by Powell and his men in mapping the area), and now, "those rags are *way* up high in those trees."

The Tabuats Ute were one of the "Northern" Ute bands (a term used by anthropologists to distinguish the Ute bands of eastern Utah and northwestern Colorado from the "Southern" Ute bands of southern and southwestern Colorado. (See fig. 15.) The Tabuats, like other Northern Utes, were excellent horsemen. They lived in skin tipis and ventured annually out onto the High Plains east of the Rocky Mountains to hunt buffalo and sometimes to contest for the buffalo grounds with the Cheyenne, Arapaho, and other Plains tribes.

In later years, Powell again worked briefly with various Northern Ute. During a horseback trip from the Uintah Indian Agency to Gunnison, Utah, Powell fell in with a Ute band, travelled with them, and spent the evenings around the campfire learning more of their language. In the summer of 1874, after he had completed his geological studies in the Uinta Mountains, he went to the Uintah Agency for a few days to gather more information on the Ute language. In the winter of 1875 he brought Richard Komas, a Northern Ute youth who was a student at Lincoln College in Pennsylvania, to Washington, D.C., for a time to continue his studies of the language.

In 1870, Powell, accompanied by Jacob Hamblin, the famed Mormon missionary to the Indians, visited the Kaibab, Uinkarets, and Shivwits bands of Southern Paiute who lived on the plateaus along the North Rim of the Grand Canyon. These peoples were close linguistic relatives of the Ute but had few horses or guns and were still living the old, pre-horse way of life.

Later the same year, Powell and Hamblin crossed the Colorado River and visited the Hopi mesas, or the Province of Tusayan, as Powell (1875b) called it in an article he wrote a few years later. During the same trip, Powell and Hamblin met with various Navajo Indians in an attempt to bring peace between them and the Mormons (Creer, 1958).

During the winter of 1871–72 and again in 1872–73, Powell's party camped near Kanab, Utah. Their primary task was to establish a base line for their planned topographic map of the Utah-northern Arizona region. But there was a band of Kaibab Indians nearby (figs. 1, 16, and 17), and at every opportunity, Powell recorded myths and tales and vocabulary items and took down other information about the customs of the people (figs. 2 and 17). When he could, he took Indians along as guides and packers on his trips across the country and continued his inquiries around the fire in the evenings.

In 1873, Powell and G. W. Ingalls were appointed Special Commissioners for the Department of Indian Affairs to investigate the "conditions and wants" of the Indians of the Canyon Country and the adjacent Great Basin (Powell and Ingalls,

FIGURE 1.—Kaibab Paiute Indians. *Left:* Woman making basket, Kaibab Plateau. *Right:* Man posed working on chipped stone knife, near Kanab, Utah. Photographs by J. K. Hillers, 1873, from Smithsonian Institution, Bureau of American Ethnology Collection.

1874). In the course of this investigation, lasting from May until early November 1873, Powell was able to contact representatives of most of the Indian groups in Utah, Nevada, and northern Arizona. Many of them came to a meeting held outside Salt Lake City, Utah, in May. Later in the summer, Powell and Ingalls travelled through central and southern Utah and met with various Indian bands or their representatives. In September, a second general meeting was held outside St. George, Utah (fig. 3). Powell and Ingalls then continued southwestward to Las Vegas and into southeastern California before turning back to Salt Lake City.

In addition to learning of the "conditions and wants" of the Indians, Powell collected a good deal of ethnographic and linguistic information. From Naches (fig. 4), a son of the famed Chief Winnemucca of the Northern Paiute (Paviotso) of Nevada, Powell collected stories, vocabularies, and data on kinship. From others, such as Seguit, a Gosiute from Skull Valley, Utah, and from Kanosh, the chief of the Pahvant Ute near Fillmore, Utah, Powell collected vocabularies, lists of leaders of Indian bands, myths, and tales (Fowler and Fowler, 1969b).

John K. ("Jack") Hillers accompanied Powell and Ingalls during their investigations. Hillers had joined Powell's second river expedition as a boatman. After E. O. Beaman, the photographer for the party, left at Kanab in 1872, Hillers became the official photographer for the Powell survey. He was to remain associated with Powell as photographer for the Rocky Mountain Survey and, later, the U.S. Geological Survey until 1900.

During the 1873 trip, Hillers took photographs of the Indians, especially of the Southern Paiute. Many of the photographs, now in the Smithsonian Institution, show authentic details of Indian customs and have been studied with profit by anthropologists (Steward, 1939; Euler, 1966b). On the other hand, some of the photographs are not ethnographically accurate. Powell was interested in pro-

FIGURE 2.—Powell (on right) meeting with Kaibab Paiutes, Kaibab Plateau, 1873. White man to left of Powell may be Jacob Hamblin. Photograph by J. K. Hillers, from Smithsonian Institution, Bureau of American Ethnology Collection.

FIGURE 3.—The Powell-Ingalls Special Commission meeting with Southern Paiutes near St. George, Utah, September 1873 (Powell standing on left). Photograph by J. K. Hillers, from Smithsonian Institution, Bureau of American Ethnology Collection.

FIGURE 4.—Naches, one of Powell's Northern Paiute informants, 1873. Photograph from National Archives, Bureau of Indian Affairs Collection.

FIGURE 5.—Southern Paiute women wearing Ute dresses. Women are wearing baskets for seed gathering and are carrying winnowing trays. Photograph by J. K. Hillers, 1873, from Smithsonian Institution, Bureau of American Ethnology Collection.

ducing stereopticon views for sale. Apparently in order to appeal to easterners' preconceptions of what Indians "ought" to look like, Powell had brought with him various articles of clothing which he had earlier collected from the Ute of the White River area. These clothes, together with some feather headdresses, apparently made to order for the occasion by the Indians under Ellen Thompson's[5] direction, were used to dress up the Southern Paiute to look more like "Indians." In addition, many of the poses are very stylized (fig. 6). The women in figure 5 are Southern Paiute from the Kaibab Plateau in northern Arizona, but the dresses are of Northern Ute manufacture from northwestern Colorado.

Powell had a number of such pictures made into stereopticon views, which were very popular items in 19th-century American drawing rooms. He sold many sets of the views showing the Indians and the geological features in Utah and Arizona. A rumor among Powell's employees in Washington, D.C., in the 1880's was that the mortgage on the Powell home at 910 M Street, N.W., was largely paid off by the sale of the views. Powell also gave away many sets to Congressmen and other Government officials. Thus, many people in the East learned something about the Indians of the Canyon Country, even though the Indians were sometimes dressed in other people's clothing.

During the latter half of the 1870's, Powell devoted most of his time to administration. He found little time to continue his studies of the Indians, but his interest in Indians continued and broadened. He envisioned a Government agency devoted to the study of American Indian cultures, past and present. He began moving in that direction in 1876 by hiring the Reverend J. Owen Dorsey and Albert S. Gatschet as "philologists" attached to the Rocky Mountain Survey. Dorsey had been a missionary to

---

[5] Ellen Thompson was Powell's sister. Her husband, Almon H. Thompson, served for several years in the 1870's as Powell's chief cartographer and second in command. He later worked for the U.S. Geological Survey.

FIGURE 6.—*Left:* Posed group of Kaibab Paiute men. Chuarumpeak, leader of Kaibab band who accompanied Powell on a number of trips, is on left. *Right:* Powell, dressed in Indian clothing, with Ute woman, probably in Uinta basin. Photographs by J. K. Hillers, 1873 (left) and 1874 (right), from Smithsonian Institution, Bureau of American Ethnology Collection.

the Ponca Indians of Iowa. Gatschet had earlier worked for the Hayden survey. Both men continued to work with Powell on anthropological matters for many years.

Throughout the 1870's there had been increasing agitation to do away with the overlapping work of the four "great surveys." Finally, in 1879, the Powell, Hayden, and Wheeler surveys were abolished and the United States Geological Survey was established. Fieldwork by the King survey had been completed in 1873. At this time, Powell got his chance to form an "ethnological" bureau to study the American Indians. The bill that created the Geological Survey also contained a clause providing for the completion of the unfinished ethnological work of the Powell survey. This was to be carried out under the auspices of the Smithsonian Institution and Powell was named to direct the work. In succeeding years, new appropriations were forthcoming. Thus, the Bureau of Ethnology (after 1894, the Bureau of American Ethnology) was created. Powell remained Director of the Bureau until his death in 1902.

After 1879, Powell was able to make only one brief trip to study the Indians in the West. In the fall of 1880, he journeyed to eastern California to collect myths and tales from the Wintun Indians. On his way back to Washington, D.C., he stopped at Pyramid Lake, Battle Mountain, and Winnemucca in Nevada to gather data on the Northern Paiute and Western Shoshoni (Fowler and Fowler, 1969b).

In 1881, Powell became the Director of the Geological Survey, while retaining his position in the Bureau of Ethnology. After that, his increasing administrative duties precluded any further fieldwork, although he did manage to visit his men in the field occasionally and to accompany them on brief visits to archeological sites or to various Indian villages.

THE ARCHEOLOGY OF THE CANYON COUNTRY

By Robert C. Euler

A century ago, Powell was concerned primarily with the investigation of then largely unknown territory and the description of its geological features His interest in the aboriginal inhabitants was relegated to a somewhat secondary role. Powell often speculated about the prehistoric ancestors of these native tribes, but he rarely deviated from his major goals in order to make detailed or extensive examinations of prehistoric settlements that so abundantly dotted the landscape.

In his 36-page report on explorations in 1873 in the vicinity of Grand Canyon, for example, Powell (1874, p. 33) devoted 7½ pages to ethnology and but one paragraph to "Antiquities." The rest of that report is of a geological nature. The archeological paragraph mentions prehistoric people who built stone or adobe houses, cultivated the soil, and had some ceramic art. Powell's succinct summary notes only that "The ruins of many of these houses have been discovered in the valley of the Colorado [River], and in them broken pottery, stone implements, and baskets have been found."

It is not too surprising, then, that during their two voyages through the Grand Canyon in 1869 and 1872, Powell and his men paid only scant attention to the nature of the prehistoric ruins they found. Often, in fact, many of the diarists of the party failed to mention them at all. On both trips only eight ruins were recorded in Grand Canyon and a few others were recorded upriver. This is not meant to be a hypercritical comment; Powell's task was one of primary exploration. In view of this and the hardships he faced, his lack of concern with prehistory is understandable.

Later explorers, such as Robert Brewster Stanton, who in 1889–90 surveyed a water-level railroad route through Grand Canyon, noted a few additional archeological sites. It was not until later, in the 20th century, that professional archeologists began systematic surveys. Investigations by Judd (1926), Haury (1932), Hall (1942), and Wilder (1944) added considerable data, especially about prehistoric sites on the rims of the canyon.

No trained archeologist retraced Powell's river route, however, until 1953 when Walter Taylor (1958) conducted a survey in the inner gorges of Marble and Grand Canyons. This was followed by more intensive reconnaissance by Schwartz (1960, 1963, 1965) and the present author (Euler, 1966a, 1967; Euler and Taylor, 1966; McNutt and Euler, 1966).

More than 250 sites below the rims of the canyon, 37 of them directly along Powell's river routes below Lees Ferry, have now been recorded.[6] From these surveys, a rather clear picture of the nature of the prehistoric human utilization of Grand Canyon has been drawn (Euler, 1967).

Some time between 3,000 and 4,000 years ago, hunting and gathering peoples, perhaps associated with the Pinto Basin-Desert Culture Complex, made and deposited split-twig animal effigies in isolated caves in the Mississippian limestone formation deep within the canyon. These, presumably, were acts of imitative magic to give ritual assurance of success in the hunt. The Pinto Basin affinities of these people remain hypothetical and are based on the discovery of diagnostic Pinto projectile points, probably made about the same time, on Red Butte near the South Rim of Grand Canyon (Euler and Olsen, 1965; McNutt and Euler, 1966).

From that archaic period until about A.D. 700, the canyon was apparently uninhabited by human groups. Then, small clusters of Anasazi (Pueblo) Indian farmers, probably ancestral to the Hopi, began to settle on the rims and in tributary canyons below. The Anasazi incursions, from the east, continued to be sporadic until about A.D. 1100. About this time, for reasons not yet clear, there was a greater influx of Puebloan peoples, culminating about A.D. 1150. Most of the archeological sites within Grand Canyon, and all but one recorded by the Powell parties, are of this period. They represent Anasazi affiliated with the Kayenta branch east of the great gorge. The Kayenta people, in turn, were closely related to the Virgin, Mesa Verde, and Chaco branches of the Anasazi (fig. 7).

Most of Grand Canyon was abandoned by the Pueblos toward the end of this period, again for reasons that remain obscure. Only occasionally, and after A.D. 1300, did Anasazi venture into the canyon, primarily the eastern section, in search of salt from the now well-known deposits below the mouth of the Little Colorado River.

---

[6] In this paper, a site may be considered to be any lasting evidence of human utilization, from a group of surface potsherds marking a former campsite to the clusters of ruined masonry structures such as those recorded at Unkar or Nankoweap deltas. Each site is recorded in the Prescott College Archaeological Survey and is given in this paper in brackets; for example, [Ariz. C:13:4 (PC)].

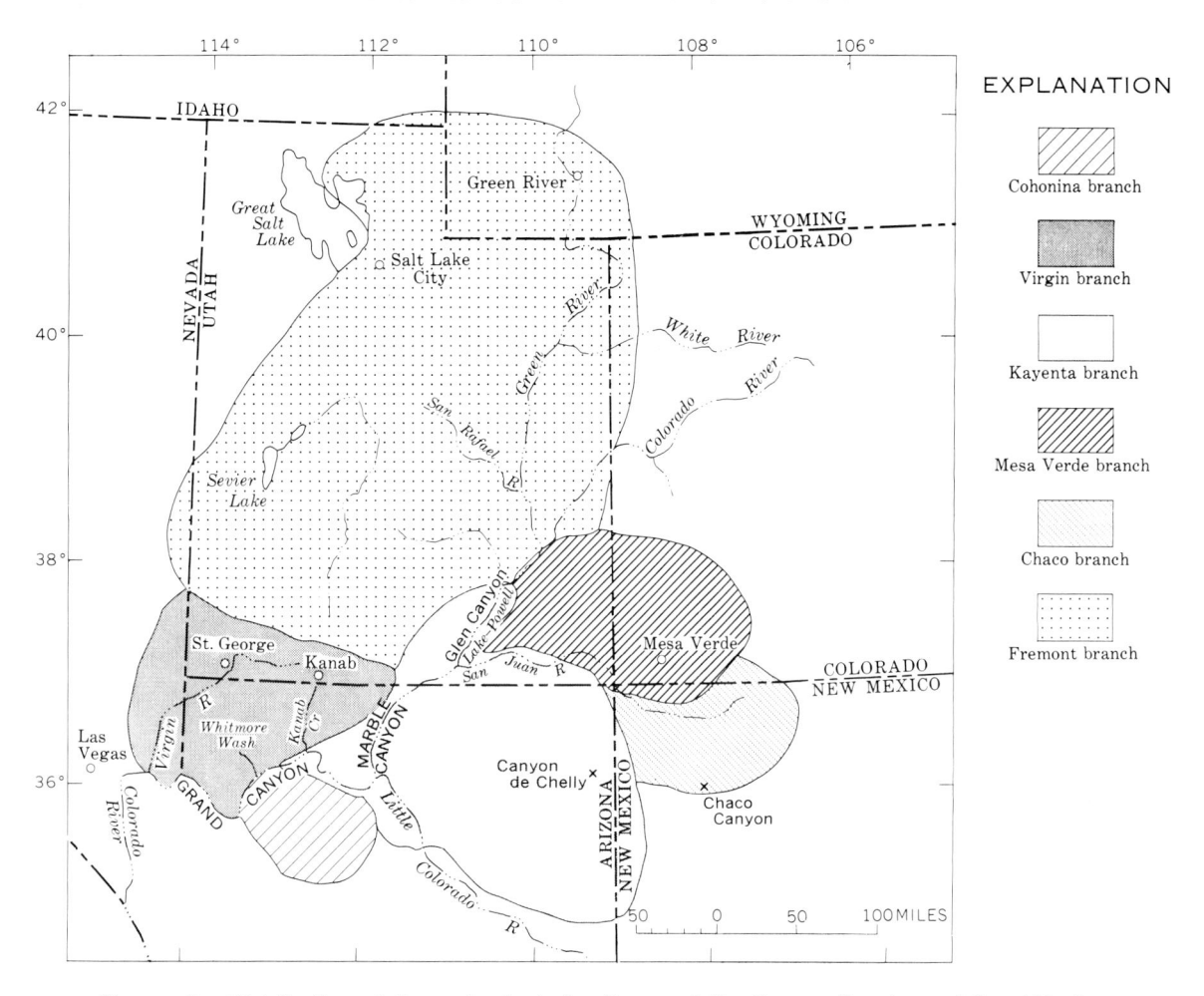

FIGURE 7.—Distribution of the archeological cultures of the Canyon Country and Great Basin.

Soon after A.D. 1150, ancestors of the Southern Paiute apparently moved into the canyon in small numbers from the north and occupied a few rock shelters and an occasional abandoned Pueblo ruin in the North Rim tributaries. During the same period, some ancestors of the Pai (Walapai and Havasupai Indians) moved into the canyon from the South Rim. They also favored rock shelters and carried on a similar farming-hunting-gathering subsistence. The Paiute and the Pai occupations, albeit by small numbers of families, continued until the 1880's when their range was restricted by governmental fiat, and they were removed to nearby reservations.

The Indian occupation was followed, in turn, by that of a few hardy prospectors searching for copper, lead, and asbestos. Their mine shafts and cabins, built in the two decades immediately preceding and following the opening of the 20th century, are occasionally found in Grand Canyon and, in at least one instance, explain the reconstruction of a prehistoric Anasazi "cliff dwelling." Those historic habitations, however, were in use after Major Powell's initial exploration a century ago.

During the first river trip, the party stopped briefly at the confluence of the Green and San Rafael Rivers. Powell (1895, p. 199) reported that: "Here we stop for an hour or two and take a short walk up the valley, and find it is a frequent resort for Indians. Arrowheads are scattered about, many of them very beautiful; flint chips are strewn over the ground in great profusion, and the trails are well worn."

So far as is known, this site has not been revisited.

Further downriver at the head of Glen Canyon, the party found two ruins (Powell, 1895, p. 227–228): "*July 29*—We enter a canyon today, with low, red walls. A short distance below its head we discover the ruins of an old building on the left wall. There is a narrow plain between the river and the wall just here, and on the brink of a rock 200 feet high stands this old house. Its walls are of stone, laid in mortar with much regularity. It was probably built three stories high; the lower story is yet almost intact; the second is much broken down, and scarcely anything is left of the third. Great quantities of flint chips are found on the rocks near by, and many arrowheads, some perfect, others broken; and fragments of pottery are strewn about in great profusion. On the face of the cliff, under the building and along down the river for 200 or 300 yards, there are many etchings. * * * We run down fifteen miles farther, and discover another group. The principal building was situated on the summit of the hill. A part of the walls are standing, to the height of eight or ten feet, and the mortar yet remains in some places. The house was in the shape of an L, with five rooms on the ground floor—one in the angle and two in each extension. In the space in the angle there is a deep excavation. From what we know of the people in the Province of Tusayan [the Hopi country of northern Arizona], who are, doubtless, of the same race as the former inhabitants of these ruins, we conclude that this was a *kiva*, or underground chamber in which their religious ceremonies were performed."

The first ruin (fig. 8) stands on a ledge overlooking the modern settlement of White Canyon, Utah, across the Colorado River from the Hite ferry and was occupied by the Anasazi about A.D. 1100 (Weller, 1959, p. 603).

The second ruin, at the mouth of Red Canyon, was excavated in 1958–59 by the University of Utah (Lipe, 1960) and named "Loper Ruin" after Bert Loper who built a cabin near the ruin in 1910 and lived there for many years. The site was of Mesa Verde Anasazi affinities of the early Pueblo III stage. Powell's suspicions of a kiva were confirmed, although the excavations revealed that it had never been completed (Lipe, 1960, p. 132). Both ruins are now submerged beneath the waters of Lake Powell.

A few miles below the second ruin, Powell and his men camped for the night. Powell (1895, p. 229) wrote:

FIGURE 8.—Ruin on ledge near mouth of White Canyon, Utah. Photograph from Department of Anthropology, University of Utah, Salt Lake City, Utah.

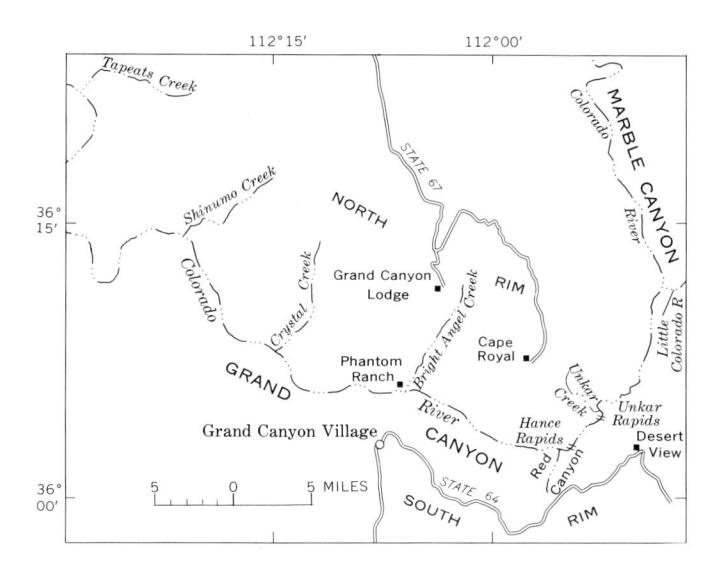

FIGURE 9.—Eastern part of Grand Canyon, Ariz.

"Just before sundown I attempt to climb a rounded eminence, from which I hope to obtain a good outlook on the surrounding country. It is formed of smooth mounds, piled one above another. Up these I climb, winding here and there to find a practicable way, until near the summit they become too steep for me to proceed. I search about a few minutes for an easier way, when I am surprised at finding a stairway, evidently cut in the rock by hands. At one place, where there is a vertical wall of 10 or 12 feet, I find an old, rickety ladder. It may be that this was a watchtower of that ancient people whose homes we have found in ruins. On many of the tributaries of the Colorado, I have * * * examined their deserted dwellings. Those that show evidences of being built during the latter part of their occupation of the country are usually placed on the most inaccessible cliffs. Sometimes the mouths of the caves have been walled across, and there are many other evidences to show their anxiety to secure defensible positions. Probably the nomadic tribes were sweeping down upon them and they resorted to these cliffs and canyons for safety. It is not unreasonable to suppose that this orange mound was used as a watchtower."

Powell and his companions passed on through Glen Canyon without making further note of other archeological sites.

After Powell and his men left Lees Ferry on August 5, 1869, they reported no ruins (although some have since been found on the route) throughout the entire 61½ miles of Marble Canyon. It was not until they reached the mouth of the Little Colorado River, the arbitrary beginning of Grand Canyon (fig. 9), that the first mention was made of an archeological site. Powell noted in his journal that they reached the Flax River, as he called the Little Colorado, on August 11 (Darrah, 1947, p. 129). In his usual terse style he remarked: "Old Indian camp seen, trails footpaths." In his lengthier and somewhat controversial account (Powell, 1875a, p. 77–78), he elaborated:

"I walk down the gorge to the left at the foot of the cliff, climb to a bench, and discover a trail, deeply worn in the rock. Where it crosses the side gulches, in some places, steps have been cut. I can see no evidence of its having been traveled for a long time. It was doubtless a path used by the people who inhabited this country anterior to the present Indian races—the people who built the communal houses * * *.

"I return to camp about three o'clock, and find that some of the men have discovered ruins, and many fragments of pottery; also, etchings and hieroglyphics on the rocks."

George Bradley, one of Powell's chief boatmen on the trip, corroborated this observation, but in so doing, confused the identification of the prehistoric people. He noted in his journal entry of August 10, 1869 (Darrah, 1947, p. 61): "There are signs of Indians here but quite old. Cannot tell whether they are Moquis [Hopis] or Apaches. I think more likely the latter for the Moquis keep close to their villages." Bradley, of course, was unaware that this campsite and trail were well known to the Hopi who frequented it on their journeys to the salt deposits only about a mile down the Colorado River.

When Major Powell again camped at this spot on his second voyage in 1872, he made no mention of the ruin. Two of his companions, Stephen Jones and Walter C. Powell, the Major's young cousin, however, wrote briefly about it. Jones, on August 23 of that year (H. E. Gregory, in Darrah and others, 1948–49, p. 147), remarked: "Up the Flax [Little Colorado] are old trails. Probably the Co-o-me-nes [Cosninas, an early name for Havasupai] and perhaps the Navajos had been here." Walter Powell (Charles Kelly, in Darrah and others, 1948–49, p. 441), on the same date, simply noted "an old fireplace on Indian trail found near camp."

Walter Taylor (1958, p. 23) tried unsuccessfully to locate this ruin in 1953. In my first reconnaissance in 1960 (Euler and Taylor, 1966, p. 29), I noted a small, one-room stone cabin a short distance above the mouth of the Little Colorado, but the construction and the artifacts within it were of recent historic vintage. According to Daniel E. Davis:[7]

"Only one person is known to have lived in the Lower Little Colorado, a prospector named Ben Beamer. He built a stone house under an overhanging ledge of Tapeats sandstone a short distance up the Little Colorado River. Beamer first went into this area in February, 1890 via the Tanner Trail. Apparently he lived here until 1892, leaving the canyon only once during that time. The only people he saw during his entire stay was a railroad survey party in the spring of 1892. His house is still in a good state of preservation and much of his equipment is still there including a plow with which he tried to cultivate a small plot of land near his house."[8]

Numerous prehistoric potsherds were found in the face of the eroding alluvial terrace in front of Beamer's cabin during my 1960 and subsequent investigations in 1962, 1965, and 1968. It is hypothesized that Beamer, in 1889, built his cabin from the ruins of the prehistoric site that Powell's men had recorded two decades earlier.

An analysis of the ceramic materials indicates that the site [Ariz. C:13:4 (PC)] was utilized by at least three or four different ethnic groups over a long period of time before Beamer arrived on the scene. The earliest use was during the 12th century A.D. by Kayenta Anasazi peoples in an early Pueblo III stage of their culture. The site was then used by the Hopi, perhaps as early as A.D. 1300, and they continued to use the site conceivably into late historic times. At some time after A.D. 1150, the site also was visited by Southern Paiute and Pai Indians; their diagnostic pottery, probably indigenous and not representing intrusive trade ware, also has been recovered from the surface of the ruin. It is not possible to infer whether the site was in use on a more or less permanent basis or was only seasonally occupied during journeys to the salt deposits nearby. There is, to be certain, no evidence of Bradley's Apaches, who never ranged that far north, nor of Walter Powell's Navajos, who, before 1872, probably were not often seen that far west of their own territory.

Between the mouth of the Little Colorado River and Unkar Creek, some 11 miles down the Colorado (fig. 9), is the greatest concentration of Pueblo ruins to be seen anywhere along the river through Grand Canyon. Only one such site was seen by the Powell parties, although, in 1872, Frederick Dellenbaugh,

---

[7] Davis, D. E., 1959, A résumé of the scientific values and interpretive potential of the lower portion of the canyon of the Little Colorado River and its environs: unpub. ms., Grand Canyon Natl. Park, Ariz.

[8] R. C. Stanton, the railroad surveyor, did not mention seeing Beamer or his cabin when he stopped at the mouth of the Little Colorado River on January 20, 1890. Two days later and approximately 14 miles downriver, however, he met a prospector from Flagstaff, Ariz., Felix Lantier, and his dog (Stanton, 1965, p. 144–146). Davis was in error on his date and identification. Beamer's possessions noted by Davis have since been removed to the visitor center at Grand Canyon National Park for safekeeping.

FIGURE 10.—Kayenta Anasazi masonry structure opposite Unkar Creek. On August 27, 1872, Walter Powell and Almon Thompson "climbed a peak about 500 feet high * * *." and "Found an old stone house * * *" (Charles Kelly, in Darrah and others, 1948–49, p. 442). *Right:* Note loophole in upper left wall. Arrow indicates magnetic north and is 30 centimeters long. Photographs by R. C. Euler.

artist and boatman on the second expedition, recorded what may have been a Paiute hut. On August 27, while pursuing some mountain sheep in the vicinity of the Unkar delta, he noted (Dellenbaugh, 1908, p. 224) that: "Near this point there was a small abandoned hut of mesquite logs." No one has ever been able to relocate this site. My hypothesis that it may have been Southern Paiute is based upon the following points:

1. Pueblos did not construct wood houses, and even if they had, one would not have survived unscathed until the time of Dellenbaugh's visit.
2. Paiutes frequently did build wood or brush structures (Euler, 1966b).
3. Dellenbaugh was hunting on the right bank of the river, which, after A.D. 1150 was within the territory of the Southern Paiute.

Later that same day, after making camp on the opposite side of the river, Walter Powell and Almon Thompson (known to the men as "Prof.") "climbed a peak about 500 feet high * * * ." and "Found an old stone house evidently built by the Sto-ce nee nas [Cosninas]" (Charles Kelly, in Darrah and others, 1948–49, p. 442). This is the only description given by any of Powell's party on either expedition of a large, well-preserved one-room masonry structure located on a high bluff opposite the mouth of Unkar Creek (fig. 10, left

FIGURE 11.—Ruins at the mouth of Bright Angel Creek discovered by Powell on August 16, 1869: "Late in the afternoon I * * * discover the ruins of two or three old houses * * *. Only the foundations are left * * *" (Powell, 1895, p. 259). Arrow indicates magnetic north and is 30 centimeters long. Photograph by R. C. Euler.

FIGURE 12 (above and right).—On August 17, 1869, camped at the confluence of Crystal Creek and the Colorado River, Powell wrote, "Grand scenery. Old Indian camps" (Darrah, 1947, p. 130). *Above:* Arrow points to site of ruins which is on a gravel terrace remnant of the Crystal Creek delta. *Right:* One of the four Pueblo masonry ruins. Photographs by R. C. Euler.

photo).[9] As reported earlier (Euler and Taylor, 1966, p. 41), this coursed masonry room is 3.6 meters wide, 8.5 meters long, and has walls that still stand to a height of almost 2 meters. Two or three small rectangular openings near the top of the walls resemble loopholes. The site appears today (fig. 10, right photo) in much the same condition as it did when Stanton photographed it in 1890. It commands an extensive view in all directions and lies on what probably was a cross-canyon trail from the Pueblo villages in the Unkar vicinity up to the South Rim of the canyon. An analysis of its surface ceramics would indicate that it was not a Cosninas, or Havasupai, site, but was utilized by the Kayenta Anasazi in an early Pueblo III stage about A.D. 1100–1150 and may have been a "lookout" if not a defensive unit. There is no evidence for overt hostility in Grand Canyon.

On Major Powell's first trip in 1869, the party entered the Precambrian "granite" for the first time on the evening of August 13. This was about 15 miles below the mouth of the Little Colorado at what is now known as Hance Rapid where Red Canyon joins the Colorado (fig. 9). The Major noted cryptically in his journal, "Ind. camp nearby" (Darrah, 1947, p. 129). This campsite is probably the one in the sand dunes on the right bank of Red Canyon, a short distance from its mouth. Although the site [Ariz. C:13:5 (PC)] is today badly eroded, it consists of five small sherd areas, each about 3 meters in diameter. Each also is marked by charcoal-stained sand and burned, fire-cracked rocks. An

---
[9] [Ariz. C:13:2 (PC)]. We (Euler and Taylor, 1966, p. 41) earlier thought that this site had first been discovered by Stanton in 1890. Closer interpretation of W. C. Powell's journal leads us to believe that he and Thompson first saw it in 1872.

analysis of the sherds indicates an occupation by Kayenta Anasazi of an early Pueblo III stage (about A.D. 1100–1150), who probably came down to the river on a trail through Red Canyon from the South Rim.

When the 1869 expedition reached the mouth of what Powell at first called Silver Creek (Darrah, 1947, p. 130) and later, Bright Angel Creek (Powell, 1875a, p. 87), he belatedly mentioned that he had "(Found some [Indian] remains at Silver Creek) (and Mill)." In his expanded 1895 publication (p. 259), he gave more details. His entry for August 16, 1869, reveals:

"Late in the afternoon I return, and go up a little gulch, just above this creek, about 200 yards from camp, and discover the ruins of two or three old houses, which were originally of stone laid in mortar. Only the foundations are left, but irregular blocks, of which the houses were constructed, lie scattered about. In one room I find an old mealing stone [the "mill" of his first journal], deeply worn, as if it had been much used. A great deal of pottery is strewn around, and old trails, which in some places are deeply worn into the rocks, are seen." Powell then attempted to interpret these ruins (fig. 11), and he wondered why the inhabitants chose such inaccessible places for their homes. He suggested that they were an agricultural people but had no lands to farm, although he also drew a parallel with the Hopi terraced gardens at the village of Moenkopi, Ariz., east of Grand Canyon. Then, without the time perspective we have today, he suggested that the Indians who had occupied the Bright Angel site fled into the canyon from the Spaniards.

Other members of Powell's party in 1869, and again on the second trip in 1872, noted these ruins. Bradley, writing on August 16, 1869 (Darrah, 1947, p. 65), remarked that "There is another old Moqui ruin where we are camped tonight. Have found the same little fragments of broken crockery as we did before." Three years later, on August 31, 1872, Stephen Jones wrote briefly (H. E. Gregory, in Darrah and others, 1948–49, p. 150) that he "Found Shinumos ruins at mouth of Bright Angel

FIGURE 13 (above and right).—Ruins above mouth of Shinumo Canyon discovered by Powell on August 20, 1869. *Above:* "Here on a terrace of trap, we discover another group of ruins." (Powell, 1875a, p. 90). Photograph by George Wharton James, 1899, courtesy of Southwest Museum, Los Angeles, Calif. Arrows point to the ruins. *Right:* Closeup view of one of the ruins. Note the metate and mano on the large rock inside the room. Arrow indicates magnetic north and is 30 centimeters long. Photograph by R. C. Euler.

Creek." Shinumo was an alternate term that Major Powell used in reference to Pueblo ruins. Walter Powell, the following day from the same camp, noted in his journal (Charles Kelly, in Darrah and others, 1948–49, p. 445) that they "Found the remains of some Moquis houses near by with some of their mills for grinding corn."

This site [Ariz. B:16:1 (PC)] was rediscovered" in 1953 by Taylor (1958, p. 22) alongside the present trail that leads from the north end of the suspension bridge across the river to Phantom Ranch. It is only a few meters above the high-water mark of the river and consists of three coursed masonry rooms. In the cliffs above are some small masonry granaries, and atop a towering, almost vertical pinnacle on the right bank of Bright Angel Creek a few hundred meters south is a small, single masonry room. The ceramic evidence from the structures near the river again indicates an early Pueblo III Kayenta Anasazi occupation, abandoned about A.D. 1150, long before the first Spaniard viewed the Grand Canyon in 1540. The only possibility of level land for agricultural pursuits nearby consists of the rock-studded sand dunes of the Bright Angel delta. A few miles up this creek, however, where the canyon widens from the narrow walled defile in Precambrian rock, are several sites of the same cultural affiliation, with ample room to accommodate the small agricultural plots that the Pueblos would have cultivated. These locations, like so many others in Grand Canyon chosen by the Anasazi for their homesites, probably did not seem inaccessible to them. On the contrary, they provided access to game such as mountain sheep, edible plants such as mesquite beans, and a long, relatively frost-free growing season for their crops of beans, squash, and corn, none of which was available to them on the rims of the canyon 4,500 to 5,700 feet above.

In the hot, rainy August of 1869, Powell and his men, after making new oars at their camp on Bright Angel Creek, continued their trip and made 10¼ miles on August 17. That evening, at their camp (No. 33), at a side canyon just above a rapid, the Major wrote: "Walk up creek 3 miles. Grand scenery. Old Indian camps" (Darrah, 1947, p. 130). The only place this could refer to is the mouth of Crystal Creek, exactly 10¼ miles below Bright Creek Angel (fig. 9). Although there are some ruins in the Crystal Creek drainage, all are more than 3 miles from its mouth. However, perched on a gravel terrace remnant of the Crystal Creek delta (fig. 12) are four single-roomed masonry dwellings [Ariz. B:16:3 (PC)], and I believe this is the site to which Powell referred. The rooms are roughly circular, ranging from 2.30 to 4.10 meters in diameter, and are constructed of slabs of Vishnu Schist, the only building rock available in this inner gorge of the canyon. The structures are set back close to the cliff and away from the precipitous terrace face that drops sheerly to the river below. Only nine pots-

herds were found when W. W. Taylor and I, after receiving word of the location of the site from Otis Marston, recorded it in 1965. Five of these were of Kayenta Anasazi affinities, whereas the rest were associated with the very similar Virgin branch of the same culture. All seemed to place the occupation in the early Pueblo III stage, again dating in this area between A.D. 1100 and A.D. 1150.

By August 20, 1869, 4 days later and just slightly more than 20 miles downriver from Bright Angel Creek, Major Powell reported another prehistoric ruin (fig. 13). The party had run through some vicious rapids, made several portages, and was enduring torrential rains. They camped in a little alcove on the right bank of the river, and Powell (1875a, p. 90) set down what for him was a lengthy description:

"Here, on a terrace of trap, we discover another group of ruins. There was evidently quite a village on this rock. Again we find mealing stones, and much broken pottery, and up in a little natural shelf in the rock, back of the ruins, we find a globular basket, that would hold perhaps a third of a bushel. It is badly broken, and, as I attempt to take it up, it falls to pieces. There are many beautiful flint chips, as if this had been the home of an old arrow maker."

Powell's original 1869 field diary (Darrah, 1947, p. 130) was considerably briefer. "Found remains of old Moquis village on bank, stone houses and pottery * * * " reads his only entry. John Sumner, one of the Major's most trusted companions on that first trip, was the only other member of the party to jot down a note about these ruins in his journal. He recorded the location simply by writing on August 20, "Camped on north side near a lot of Moqui ruins" (Darrah, 1947, p. 120). Powell stopped at the same place on his 1872 trip and, in his recently located field journal for that trip (Fowler and Fowler, 1969a), he noted on September 3, that they "Camped for dinner at the Shinumo Ruins above the deep side gulch."

This "deep side gulch" was Shinumo Canyon (fig. 9) and the "terrace of trap" on which the ruins were discovered is scarcely half a mile upriver and on the north or right bank. Stanton camped here in 1890 (Stanton, 1965, p. 178), and before 1900, William Bass, a prospector and early tourist guide in the canyon, had built a cableway across the river at this point on his trail to his winter camp on the Shinumo. In 1899, the noted author of the day, George Wharton James (1900, p. 197–203), photographed and described these Pueblo ruins.

This site [Ariz. B:15:1 (PC)], on the lower end of the terrace below a high hill separating the terrace from Shinumo Creek, consists of at least six single, separated, coursed masonry rooms (fig. 13). Two or three other rooms are at the upper end of the terrace about a mile upriver. Many potsherds, fragmentary flaked blades and chert chips, a mano, and two metates were found on the surface during my 1962, 1966, and 1967 visits. The masonry rooms are generally rectangular with rounded corners; they average about 3.0×3.5 meters in size and the walls are still standing to a maximum height of 1 meter. The sherd analysis indicates an occupation of about A.D. 1100–1150 by Kayenta Anasazi. This site, close by the river, was probably socially and politically allied with many sites occupied at the same time farther up the Shinumo drainage to the north, just as the sites at the mouths of Crystal and Bright Angel Creeks were similarly allied.

The Shinumo terrace site was the last prehistoric ruin mentioned by Major Powell on his first expedition. However, one other was noted in 1872. On September 6 of that year, as the second expedition neared the conclusion of its journey at Kanab Creek, Frederick Dellenbaugh wrote from its camp at the mouth of Tapeats Creek about 10 miles upriver (fig. 9): "A morning was spent at Tapeats Creek for examinations, and we found there some ancient house ruins not far up the side canyon" (Dellenbaugh, 1908, p. 240).

Tapeats Canyon boxes about one quarter of a mile from its mouth. It is narrow and precipitous in that stretch and to get above the cliffs to the upper end of the canyon requires some agile climbing over steep talus. Once above that, however, one can proceed along ledges and terraces for many miles. On the tops of some of those terraces, beginning about three quarters of a mile upstream from the mouth, are several Anasazi masonry ruins. None are found below this point in the narrower section of the canyon itself. Dellenbaugh must have been referring to at least one of those sites farther upstream when he wrote about "some ancient house ruins." The first site one finds in walking up Tapeats Canyon is a very obscure, small, one-room masonry site [Ariz. B:11:39 (PC)], partly hidden by a large boulder which forms one of its walls. This Pueblo structure is on the left side of Tapeats Creek, the side of most difficult access, and is some 50 meters above the water. Dellenbaugh was probably walking up the right bank and found a much larger structure, quite visible on the terrace [Ariz. B:11:38 (PC)]. This pueblo consists of four single and separated rooms flanking a series of approximately five contiguous storerooms (fig. 14). Again, as for the other sites mentioned here, the ceramic analysis of the many sherds collected indicates a Kayenta Anasazi occupation during an early Pueblo III stage, about A.D. 1100–1150.

The Paiute gardens that Powell saw on August 26, 1869 (Darrah, 1947, p. 131), apparently were near the mouth of Whitmore Wash. No trace of them or of a Paiute campsite at this point has been recorded. Although the Major remarked (Powell, 1875a, p. 95–96) that, "Since we left the Colorado Chiquito, we have seen no evidences that the tribes of Indians inhabiting the plateaus on either side ever come down to the river * * * ", several Paiute and Pai campsites have since been located along the river through Grand Canyon. These seem to have been small, impermanent camps, and they cannot be dated with any precision except that they must have been in use after A.D. 1150.

Although the Powell expeditions through Grand Canyon did not contribute greatly to the archeology of the Southwest, they did, through the diaries and publications that resulted from them, show that man had inhabited that seemingly inhospitable region centuries earlier. It should have been clear to the emaciated and battered explorers that those prehistoric aborigines were in many ways much better adapted to the environment than the explorers were with their rancid bacon, soggy coffee, and mildewed flour. Indeed, the more intensive recent archeological studies centered in Grand Canyon have demonstrated not only that its depths provided adequate subsistence for a people technogically at-

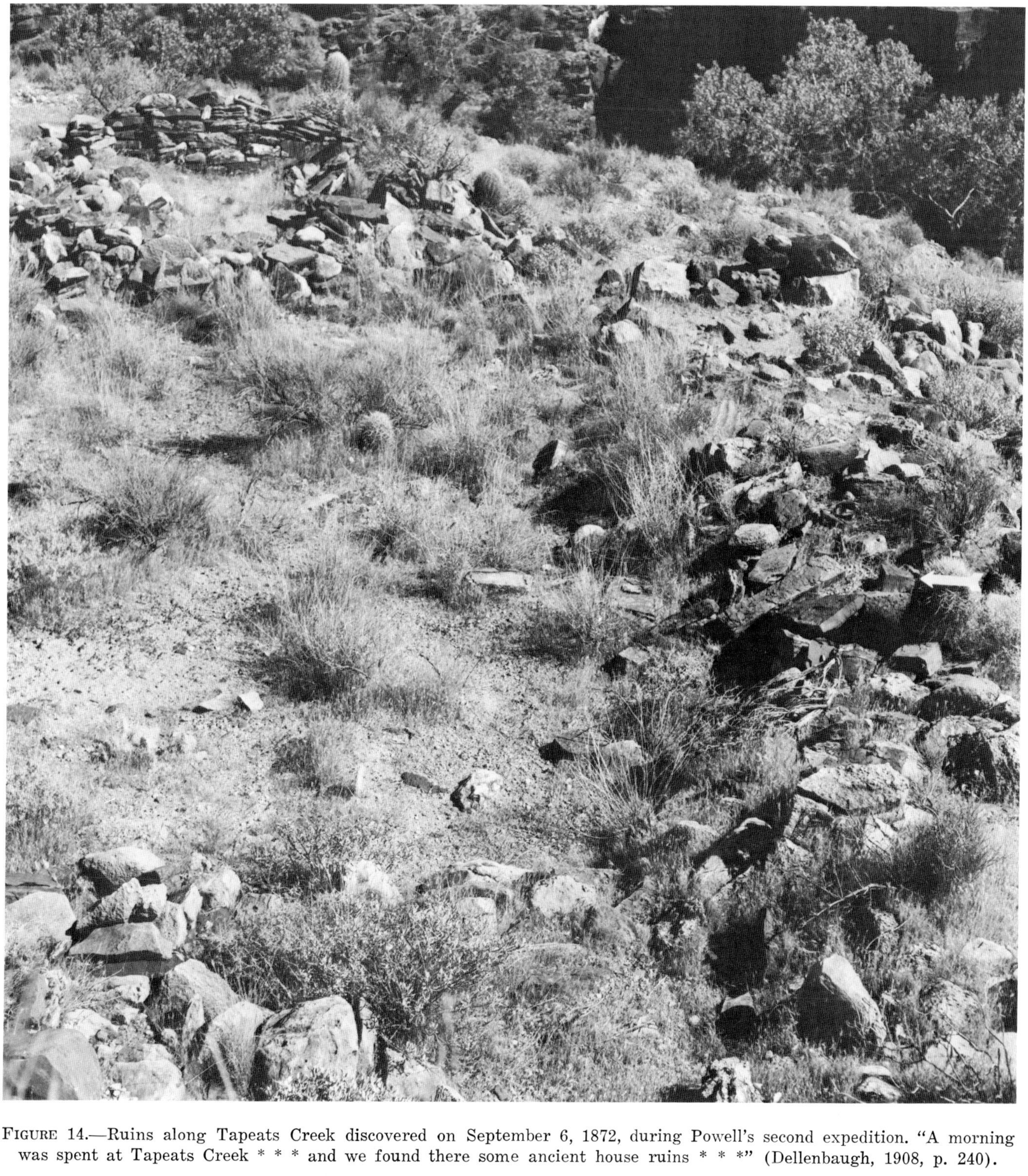

FIGURE 14.—Ruins along Tapeats Creek discovered on September 6, 1872, during Powell's second expedition. "A morning was spent at Tapeats Creek * * * and we found there some ancient house ruins * * *" (Dellenbaugh, 1908, p. 240).

tuned to their habitat, but that movement on foot through its vast recesses was entirely feasible.

THE ETHNOGRAPHY OF THE CANYON COUNTRY

By Don D. Fowler and Catherine S. Fowler

During the centuries in which the Anasazi and Fremont cultures were developing in Arizona and Utah, an older non-Pueblo way of life continued in the Great Basin in western Utah, Nevada, and southern Oregon. Archeologists call this tradition the Desert Archaic (Jennings, 1964). The climate and environment did not permit the practice of horticulture without irrigation, and the subsistence base continued to be one of foraging, hunting of animals and birds, fishing, and gathering a wide variety of seeds, roots, nuts, and insects for food.

About A.D. 1000 some of these Desert Archaic peoples who spoke Numic languages (Miller, 1966; Goss, 1968) began spreading in a fan-shaped pattern across the Great Basin from a point somewhere around Death Valley. These peoples were the ancestors of the historic tribes of the Great Basin and much of the Canyon Country (fig. 15).

The thrust of one group was along the Sierra Nevada and into southern Oregon. These people became the historic Mono and Northern Paiute (Paviotso) of western Nevada, eastern California, and southern Oregon. After horses were introduced in the 18th century, some of these people moved into southern Idaho to become the Bannock tribe of historic times (Steward, 1938).

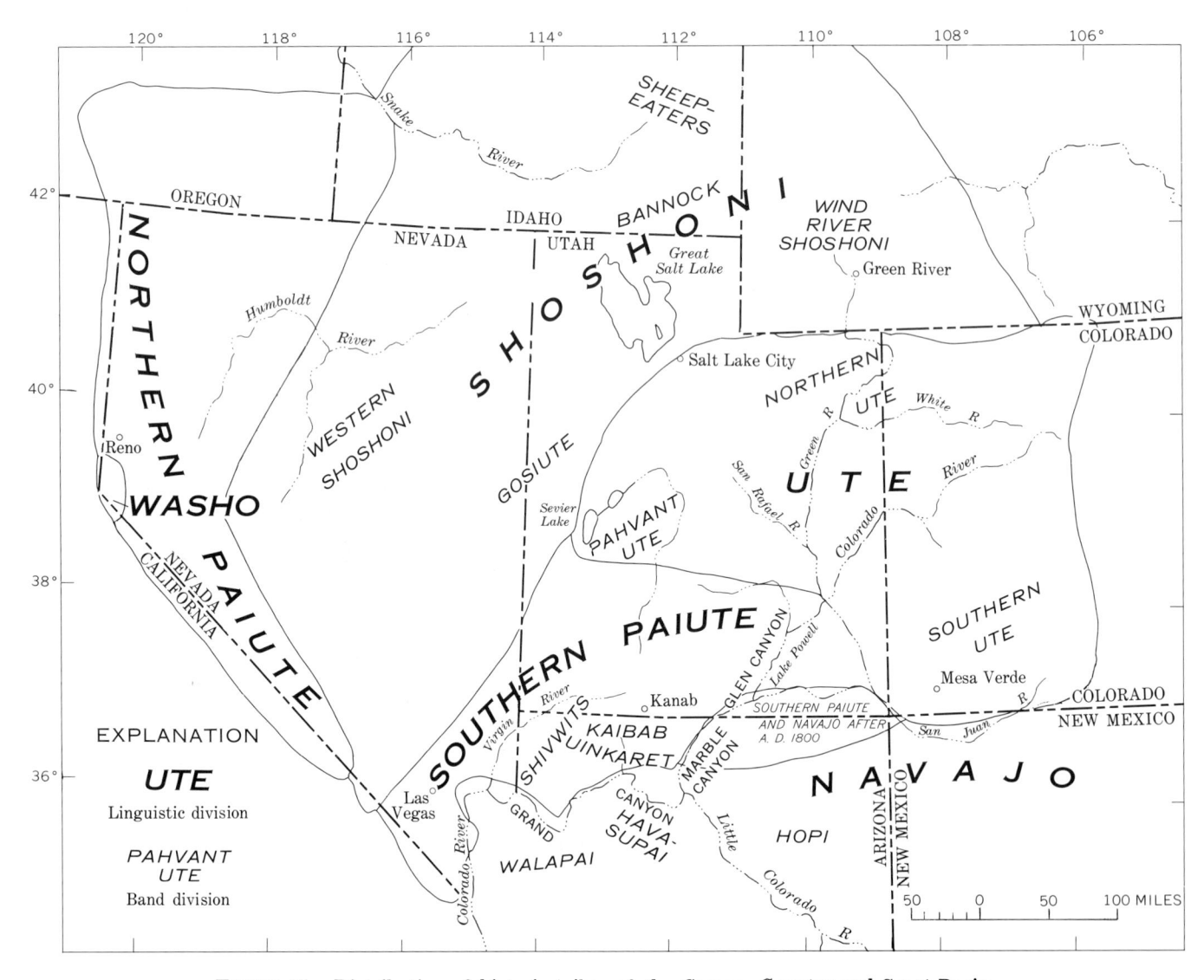

FIGURE 15.—Distribution of historic tribes of the Canyon Country and Great Basin.

A second group spread across the central part of the Great Basin to become the Western Shoshoni, the Gosiute, the "Northwestern" or "Idaho" Shoshoni (who were closely affiliated with the Bannock in the 19th century), the Lemhi and Sheepeater Shoshoni in the mountains along the Idaho-Wyoming borded, and the Wind River Shoshoni of western Wyoming (Stewart, 1958). Sometime in the late 17th or early 18th centuries, part of the Wind River Shoshoni pushed out onto the Great Plains and turned southward to become the Comanche of historic times (Shimkin, 1940).

A third group of Numic-speaking peoples spread south and east along the southern part of the Great Basin to become the historic Kawaiisu of California, the Chemehuevi of southern Nevada, and the various Ute-Southern Paiute groups of southern Nevada, southern and central Utah, and western and southern Colorado (Goss, 1968).

As noted above, the Numic-speaking peoples were carriers of the old Desert Archaic lifeway—they were foragers exploiting the available resources of an arid environment. As they pushed eastward, some of them may have encountered the Anasazi or the Fremont peoples. They may, in fact, have contributed to the withdrawal of the Anasazi or the Fremont peoples by raiding their fields and villages. The Southern Paiute may have learned farming techniques from the Anasazi peoples. In 1776, when the Southern Paiute along the Virgin River were visited by Dominguez and Escalante (Bolton, 1950), they were farming along the river bottoms. Basically, however, most of the Numic peoples, including the Southern Paiute, remained foragers.

A change for some of the Numic people, however, soon came. The Spanish began exploring the Southwest in 1540, and by the 1590's, they were well entrenched in Santa Fe and other settlements. The Spaniards brought new crops, such as wheat and peaches, to the area, as well as new animals, including sheep, burros, and the animal which had the greatest impact in the area—the horse.

By the late 1600's, the Indians around the Spanish settlements had learned to ride and care for horses. Soon the Indians began to steal horses, and horses began spreading rapidly northward to other tribes, often with the Ute, Comanche, and Wind River Shoshoni acting as intermediaries. By 1710, mounted bands of Southern Ute and Comanches were harassing the Spanish settlements. By 1750, horses had reached the northern Plains (Haimes, 1938). Many previously semisedentary, earth-lodge-dwelling farmers in that area rapidly became nomadic tipi-dwelling buffalo hunters—the true "Plains" Indians—for example, the Crow, Arapaho, Cheyenne, and others.

On the edges of the Canyon Country the Northern and the Southern Ute bands also became horsemen. They ranged through the central Rockies and out onto the high plains of Colorado, Wyoming, and even Kansas. The Indians in the Canyon Country and in the high plateaus of Utah and the Great Basin to the west, however, did not become horsemen until much later. There was little to be gained by owning horses. Few, if any, buffalo were in those areas. Furthermore, especially in the Great Basin, horses competed with the Indians for the available grasses, a primary seed-food resource. Not until the latter half of the 19th century did some of these peoples take up the use of horses and then only briefly, as an aid in preying on ranches and wagon trains.

By the time Powell visited them, the Numic-speaking peoples of the Canyon Country and the

FIGURE 16.—Tapeats, one of Powell's Southern Paiute informants, outside his house near St. George, Utah. Photograph by J. K. Hillers, 1873, from Smithsonian Institution, Bureau of American Ethnology Collection.

FIGURE 17.—Kaibab Paiute camp on Kaibab Plateau. Indians are wearing rabbit-skin blankets. Photograph by J. K. Hillers, 1873, from Smithsonian Institution, Bureau of American Ethnology Collection.

Great Basin had been in direct, if sometimes intermittent, contact with white men, or elements of their culture, for nearly 100 years. Fathers Dominguez and Escalante has passed through the area in 1776, seeking a trail to southern California (Bolton, 1950). The advent of the American fur trade in the early 19th century brought increasing contacts between whites and Indians, especially along the headwaters of the Green River (Cline, 1963). U.S. Army exploring parties began probing the area in the 1840's (Goetzmann, 1959). The Mormons began settling along the central cordillera of Utah in 1847, and the trail to the California gold country opened up the following year.

When Powell arrived in 1868, the Indian cultures were beginning to undergo a period of rapid transition. Steel and iron began replacing chipped stone for tools; pots and pans were replacing baskets and some pottery vessels; and castoff whitemen's clothes were being substituted for bark skirts and rabbit-skin robes (figs. 16 and 17).

By 1868, the Indians were rapidly being dispossessed of their lands and resources. Settlers and miners were moving in and taking over land and fencing it—an idea completely foreign to the Indians. Livestock were turned loose in most areas and rapidly depleted the grasses and other plants on which the Indians depended heavily for food. Pinyon trees, another important Indian food source, were cut down for firewood and fenceposts.

EXTRACTS FROM JOHN WESLEY POWELL'S NOTES ON THE INDIANS

As we noted above, Powell made observations on most of the Numic-speaking bands in the Canyon Country and the Great Basin, but he knew the Southern Paiute, especially the Kaibab, Shivwits, and Uinkarets bands, best. Powell learned many things from Chuarumpeak (fig. 6), the leader of the Kaibab band, who accompanied Powell on a number of trips.

Powell was the first observer to systematically record details of the customs, practices, and beliefs of many of the Indians of the Canyon Country and the Great Basin. His early observations, at a time when many of the Indian groups were first coming into contact with whitemen, are invaluable to an understanding of the Indian cultures of the Canyon Country.

Powell intended to write a general ethnographic monograph on the "Numa," as he called the Numic-speaking peoples, paying special attention to the "Ute," by which he meant the peoples we have herein called the Northern and Southern Ute and Southern Paiute. Increasing administrative and other duties, however, kept Powell from completing the task. Several manuscripts of the intended study remain in the Smithsonian Institution Department of Anthropology archives and have recently been edited and prepared for publication (Fowler and Fowler, 1969b). The following sections are taken from those manuscripts. They represent part of the material Powell prepared on the "Ute" people of the Canyon Country and are in his words.

"Means of Subsistence"

"The food of the Utes consists of a very great variety of articles such as nuts, seeds, fruits, fleshy stalks of plants, bulbs, roots, inner bark of trees; many mammals, birds, reptiles, fishes and insects. In autumn when the nuts of the piñon pine are ripening, and before they have sufficiently matured to drop from the trees, the cones containing them are gathered and thrown in the fire, where they are left until the cones are somewhat charred, and the nuts partially roasted. They are then raked from the fire and separated from the charred chaff by picking them out with the fingers when they are ready for use.

"In seasons when these are abundant, great stores are laid away, or cached, for the winter. Usually these nuts receive no further preparation, but sometimes they are slowly and thoroughly roasted in a manner which will hereafter be described in explaining the preparation of smaller seeds. The nuts thus roasted are ground and made into mush by boiling the meal in basket jars heated with hot stones. Sometimes the meal is made into cakes and baked in the ashes. Perhaps no vegetable food is more highly prized than this.

"In the region inhabited by the most southern Pai Utes two species of leguminous plants are found in great abundance; the popular names of these plants are mesquite [*Prosopis juliflora glandulosa*] and mescrew [*Prosopis pubescens*]. These shrubs bear great quantities of pods which contain small seeds like the forest locust, the pod itself though much smaller contains a saccharine substance something like the honey locust. The pods and seeds are gathered and ground together in a flour and afterward used as mush or made into cakes. Very often these cakes instead of being baked in the fire, are sun dried and kept on hand for quite a lengthy period.

"The seeds of a very great variety of weeds and grasses are used for food; the method of gathering these will first be described. They are collected chiefly by the women and children. For this purpose a large conical basket holding from two to three bushels is used; it is carried on the back with a strap over the head [fig. 5]. Into this the seeds are placed from time to time as they are collected in a smaller basket of the same shape holding about two gallons. This is carried in the left hand and the seeds are swept into it with a little fan held in the right hand.

"Sometimes where the plants bearing the seeds are very bushy the entire clump will be pulled up by the roots and is then beaten against the edge of the basket so that the seeds fall within. By these methods a large basket will be filled in one or two hours where seeds are found in abundance. The gleaner will then repair to the camp where the seeds are winnowed. This process is as follows: A gallon or more is placed in a large shallow tray and a handful or two of finely powdered charcoal or ashes sprinkled over them, and the whole is then tossed in such a manner that [as] the chaff is carried to the edge of the tray it is blown off by the wind. In this winnowing the women become quite dextrous. When the greater part of the chaff has been blown away any little remnant that may be left is blown off with the mouth. Then the ashes and charcoal dust are removed in the same way—that is by blowing with the mouth as the seeds are tossed, and the grains of charcoal are gathered on one side in a line around the bottom of the heap by deftly shaking the whole, and then raked off with the fingers. In this manner from a peck to a half a bushel of clean seed will be separated from the large basket of unwinnowed material brought in from the fields, and not infrequently a day's labor is rewarded with three or four pecks of seeds.

"The seeds are now ready to be roasted; for this purpose another and smaller tray is used in which two or three quarts are placed and about the same amount of live coals are raked from the fire into the tray. The woman then seizes the tray with both hands and tosses the whole mass in such a way that the coals are gently fanned and the seeds kept in constant motion, so that they cannot be burned. This process is continued ten or fifteen minutes until they are thoroughly roasted. Many of them swell and burst open so that the bulk is much increased and the seeds that were gray and brown and black when placed in the tray are now of a beautiful white color like a quantity of pop corn.

"When roasted in this way the seeds are ready to be ground. For this purpose two mealing stones are used, one a flat slab about fourteen by twenty inches in size called a *mar*; the other a small oblong stone more or less rounded and held in the hands: This is called a *mó-a* [fig. 18]. The woman when grinding sits on the ground sometimes with her legs stretched out at full length, but usually doubled back, so that her toes and front part of her foot are prone on the ground and her heels beside her haunches so that she does not sit upon her feet but quite down upon the ground. The *mar* is then placed between her legs, the farther edge resting on a tray called ta-kwi-o-goats. Another tray holding the roasted seeds is near by, and from it she takes a small quantity and puts it in the *mar* and rapidly grinds the seed into a meal, dextrously separating the finer from the coarser and unground seeds, and at the same time pushing the meal thus separated over the edge of the stone into the tray. Sometimes

FIGURE 18.—Kaibab Paiute woman working with metate and mano, grinding seeds into meal. Photograph by J. K. Hillers, 1873, from Smithsonian Institution, Bureau of American Ethnology Collection.

a little child sits by and slowly feeds this mill with a little horn dipper, while the woman works away singing merrily, or scolding her lord or screaming her orders to the household. Sometimes the meal is eaten without further preparation. In such a case, the tray is placed in the camp where the household gather about it, each one helping himself by taking up a small pinch with his thumb and two fingers and deftly tossing it into his mouth. Mark, I say 'tossed into his mouth' for it is quite rare that such food is placed there, as it is thrown in with a jerk.

"At other times the meal is cooked in a kind of mush, for which purpose it is placed in a basket jar, and boiled with hot stones, in which form it is usually eaten with horn spoons, without waiting for it to be cooled. It never ceased to be a matter of astonishment to me to see how this hot boiling mush could be eaten, without producing any signs of pain from burning or scalding, which seemed to be inevitable.

"A species of cactus (*opuntia*) is very abundant in some parts of the country and it bears a beautiful crimson apple; very juicy and quite luscious. The fruit is beset with minute spines which are barbed. In gathering this fruit great pains are taken to divest them of their armiture [sic], and a little brush is made of a bundle of wire grass for this purpose. When the spines are carefully brushed off the fruit is gathered into a basket and carried into camp where the juice is expressed from the pulp which is afterwards formed into rolls or large lumps and sometimes dried for winter use.

"The mesquelle [mescal or agave] is a very important article in the food of these people. The Indian name for this plant is *yant*. The season in which it is found is one of great scarcity, for it usually formed in the spring, and the regions where it is found in abundance are often called *Ta-mun Ka-ni'-ga*.

"The plant has a fleshy stalk or crown, from which spring a number of bayonet shaped leaves and from the lower part of the stalk, fine roots penetrate the ground. A large seed stalk rises from the centre of the crown, the last year of the life of the plant, which derives its chief nourishment from the store of material previously prepared in the crown. Early in the spring, before this plant starts its growth, this stalk is very rich, and it is then when it is gathered for food. The older the plant is before the stalk is started, the richer it will be found, but after the stalk is grown it is no longer valued.

"The plant is gathered by taking a sharp stick and driving it down with a large stone through the crown, and then the mesquelle is wrenched from the ground, and whilst it is yet on the stalk the bayonet leaves and rootlets are trimmed off. When five or six crowns are thus gathered on one stick they are carried into camp. There they are roasted in the ashes. When roasted the whole is composed of a treacle-like substance held together by a great number of fibres. They are placed on trays and cut into strips and the saccharine material is sucked out. I once heard a white man say that this way of eating the mesquelle was very much like sucking molasses with a straw broom.

"This food is considered a very great luxury by the Indians, and the time of gathering the *yant* is a season of great festivity. In early spring they repair to the region where it is found in abundance, and collected in great quantities. Many bushels are sometimes brought into camp by the tribe in a single day. While the women are collecting the plant the men dig a pit, and in it they build a large fire and the pit is kept full of live coals and hot ashes. Just at daybreak these embers are raked out to the sides so as to form a deep hollow in the centre and into this the crowns are thrown and covered with the coals and ashes. Stones which have been previously heated around the fire are then thrown over them, and the loose dry earth about the fire is piled over all. All this is done with some ceremony. Here the plants are allowed to remain for twenty-four hours. From time to time a woman will thrust a stick into the mound and stir it up a little as if to give vent to gases that may have generated within. At dawn the next morning the *yant* is ready for use and the little tribe gathers in a circle around the heap and sings the *yant* song and dances the *yant* dance, which lasts for an hour or more. Then the pit is opened and they have a great feast. This dancing and singing and feasting is continued until the whole pit is exhausted, and another collection is then made.

"Animal Food"

"The flesh of the grizzly bear is esteemed very highly, and the hunter who succeeds in killing one is considered a great hero. They are now killed by fire arms but the Indians aver that they were formerly killed with arrows, and they tell many stories of the prowess of their fore-fathers in attacking and killing these huge animals. It seems that all the men of the tribe turned out on such occasions.

"The flesh of the elk, antelope, mule deer, mountain sheep, beaver, otter, three or four species of rabbits, badger, prairie dog, porcupine, and some other animals are deemed to be good food. The wolf, fox, swift, mountain lion, wild cat and others are eaten only in times of great scarcity but when very hungry the Indian will refuse no kind of meat.

"The Indian as a hunter exhibits great patience and his success is due chiefly to this characteristic. He walks in a crouching attitude through the woods or over the plains with almost noiseless step. His practiced eye discovers the tracks or sees an animal at a great distance, and when the game is discovered he will walk around for a long distance to get in such a position that the deer will be to the windward. Great care is taken to crawl upon the deer so as not to frighten him, and for this purpose an Indian will often crawl upon the ground many hundred yards so managing that the little trees and bushes even, or the inequalities of the ground, will cover his approach.

"He never discharges his gun or shoots an arrow from a distance, but if the deer occupies some position so that he cannot get quite near enough to him without exposing himself he will lie down and gently wait until his position is changed, even though it may be necessary to wait in such a place for hours.

"When any large game is killed it is sometimes skinned, dressed, cut into pieces, and hung up on a tree, the hunter himself rarely carrying but a portion into camp. This is done very quickly and the Indian proceeds on the hunt. When he returns to camp, as he usually does without game he seems to be able to describe on which [tree] it is cached in such a way that the woman can go to it unerringly.

"When a party goes out to hunt in company he who may be successful in killing the game is entitled to the skin but the flesh is divided equally among all the people. When it is brought into camp, the successful hunter himself cuts up the game and sends the several portions to those persons to whom it should be given.

"Clubs, javelins, sling stones, and arrows were formerly used by the Indians in the hunt, but all these articles except the bow and arrow are now superceded by fire arms. They still use a small stick like a cane with a curved handle for the purpose of pulling rabbits from their burroughs.

"The sage plants of the territory inhabited by the Utes are the homes of vast numbers of rabbits, and they have means by which a great many of these are caught. They form a very important article of food and their skins are made into robes. The fibres of two or three species of plants are twisted into cords and with these cords large nets are made, something like a fishing seine about three feet wide and from four to six hundred yards in length. Often a number of such nets are used together. They are placed so as to enclose a semicircular piece of ground, the whole length of the combined nets often being more than half a mile. Wings of brush are then extended on either side and the whole tribe, men, women and children, turn out and surround a large space, probably several square miles, and advance concentrically toward the net beating the bushes and shouting and screaming. The rabbits are started up and they shoot at them with arrows, killing one now and then, and driving the remainder into the net where they are entangled and shot. From two or three to twenty rabbits may be caught at one drive in this way. The owner of a section of net is entitled to the skin of the rabbit caught in his portion, but the meat is divided among all the families of the tribe.

"Another little net is used. [It is] sack-like in form with its mouth pinned or staked over the burrough of the rabbit, which on coming out is entangled in the meshes of the snare.

"In seasons of the year when the skins of these rabbits are comparatively worthless for clothing, the flesh is prepared for eating by throwing the rabbit on the fire without removing the entrails or taking off the skin. The fur is soon burned off and when the body is fairly warmed through it is ready to be eaten. It is then opened and the entrails taken out. The intestines are emptied of their contents by taking the long gut between the fingers which are tightly compressed. The pouch is cut open and turned inside out. They are then put on the fire and roasted to a crisp and are considered the most desirable part of the animal except, perhaps, the brain.

"Grasshoppers and crickets form a very important part of the food of these people. Soon after they are fledged and before their wings are sufficiently developed for them to fly, or later in the season when they are chilled with cold, great quantities are collected by sweeping them up with brush brooms, or they are driven into pits, by beating the ground with sticks. When thus collected they are roasted in trays like seeds and ground into meal and eaten as mush or cakes. Another method of preparing them is to roast great quantities of them in pits filled with embers and hot ashes, much in the same manner as *yant* is prepared for consumption. When these insects are abundant, the season is one of many festivities. When prepared in this way these insects are considered very great delicacies.

"Earth worms gathered in the same way and treated as lizards are very often dried for winter use.

"Birds eggs are eaten wherever found and if incubation is nearly complete they are much preferred.

"Most of the tribes of Pai Utes still continue to cultivate the soil to a greater or lesser extent, raising *ka-mout* [Camote], corn, and squashes. The little patches of ground selected for this purpose are situated in the vicinity of springs which are utilized for purposes of irrigation. Corn is planted sometimes in the sand eighteen or twenty inches deep; two or three seeds are planted in a hole, and when the plants come up, they branch just below the ground, so that there are usually fifteen or twenty stalks and each one will often bear a small ear of corn. After planting no further attention is given to any of the crops until they are harvested.

"Doubtless in former years before the introduction of fire arms, all the Indians paid much more attention to this mode of gaining a subsistence. An old man told me this and mourned greatly the degeneracy of his people and affirmed that they were much more prosperous and happy in the old days than at the present time.

"Courtship and Marriage"

"There are two methods of marriage. One is to steal the maiden and the other is to fight for her. Even if the maiden and all her friends are willing there is always a semblance of disapproval and so it is necessary that the girl should be taken by one of three methods. There are two words for marriage, one signifying pulling, the other conquering.

"The fighting occurs when there are rivals.

"Two men desire the same girl, and it is arranged that they shall determine the matter by wager or battle.

"Each party enlists a number of his friends and that they shall determine the matter by wager or feast and dance. Then one of the suitors walks out into the plain and in boastful language challenges his rival, ending with the expression,

A-near-ti-tik-a-nump-kwaik-ai-ger
'Fighting is the tool by which I
gain my living, I tell you!'

"Then the rival steps forth boasting of his prowess, and of that of his friends and ending with the same expression A-near-ti-tik-a-nump-kwaik-ai-ger. 'Fighting is the tool by which I gain my living I tell you!' and the combat commences.

"No weapons are allowed and when either champion falls not another blow must be struck, but the conqueror immediately repeats his challenge, and another champion enters the ring, and so the fighting is continued until one or the other of the parties is conquered. Fair dealing in these contests is always inculcated, but it often happens that in the heat of the contest one or the other party does something which is considered against the rules and a general fight in terrible earnest ensues.

"The girls are invariably married very young, and when the elder sister is married, and she is always taken first, the husband is entitled to all the sisters as they grow up and come to a marriageable age. But the oldest son is also married first, and all his brothers as they come to a marriageable age are also entitled to his wives, so that a family of boys marries a family of girls, but usually a division of the girls is made among the boys, though this is not always the case. Still as they come up, he may have to fight for them, and may be willing to relinquish them without a fight, but such is usually not the case."

Mythology and Beliefs

Powell was very much interested in the myths and tales told by the Indians and in their conceptions of the spirit world. In his narrative of his trip in 1870 to the Uinkarets Plateau, he relates how he induced the Indians to tell their myths (Powell, 1875c, p. 667):

"Having finished our business for the evening, I asked if there was a 'tu-gwe-wa-gunt' in camp—that is, if there was anyone present who was skilled in relating their mythology. Chuar said that To-mor-ro-un-ti-kai, the chief of these Indians, the Uinkarets, was a very noted man for his skill in this matter; but they both objected, by saying that the season for tu-gwe-nai had not yet arrived. [Tales were usually told only in wintertime.] But I had anticipated this, and soon some members of the party came with pipes and tobacco, a large kettle of coffee, and a tray of biscuits, and after sundry ceremonies of pipe-lighting and smoking, we all feasted; and, warmed up by this (to them unusual) good living, it was decided that the night should be spent in relating mythology."

Powell gathered many myths and tales from the Indians, as well as their beliefs about the country in which they lived, including explanations of the boundaries of the earth and of the topography and the peopling of the earth.

"The Boundaries of the Earth"

"The region of country inhabited by the Utes has some very remarkable topographic features, and it is necessary to bring out these in order to appreciate their ideas of the form and boundaries of the world.

"These features are towering cliffs, or bold escarpments of rock, often hundreds of miles long, and hundreds or thousands of feet high. The faces of these cliffs are in many places vertical. These cliffs are the boundaries or edges of mesas and high plateaux. This region of country is also traversed by deep chasms, the channels of the streams which drain the country. These streams usually have a great depth below the general surface of the country, often hundreds and thousands of feet. The Grand Cañon, one of the features with which they are very familiar, is from four to five thousand feet in depth, and more than two hundred miles in length, and the whole country is cut by a labyrinth of these deep gorges. The Indian name for these cliffs is *Mu-kwan-a-kunt*. The earth they believe to be bounded on the west by such a line of cliffs. That is, by going beyond the sea in this direction, you climb to a summit of a mesa and then look off from the brink of the cliffs where the world ends. They believe too that these cliffs are very treacherous, that there are projecting rocks at the summit that are delicately balanced and that too inquisitive people in looking over the brink have fallen over and gone—ah! they know not where.

"The middle of the world is the Kaibab Plateau, the home of the *Pa Utes*, or true Utes as the word signifies.

"The eastern edge of the world is a line of cliffs like that on the west. It may seem strange, but in talking with them I have never been able to obtain from them any ideas of what they supposed might be the northern and southern boundaries * * *. Their usual reply is, 'The ancients never told us about a northern and southern end to the ground.'

"The Origin of the Cañons of the Colorado"

"Many years ago when wise and good men lived on the earth, the great Chief of all the Utes lost his beloved wife.

"Day and night he grieved, and all his people were sad. Then Rabbit [Ta-vwoats] [10] (one of the dignitaries in the mythology) appeared to the chief and tried to comfort him, but his sorrow could not be allayed. So at last Rabbit promised to take him to a country away to the southwest where he said his dead wife had gone and let him see how happy she was if he would agree to grieve no more on his return. So he promised. Then Rabbit took his magical ball and rolled it before him, and as it rolled it rent the earth and mountains, and crushed the rocks and made a way for them to that beautiful land—a trail through the mountains which intervened between that home of the dead and the hunting grounds of the living. And following the ball, which was a rolling globe of fire, they came at last to the Spirit Land. Then the great Chief saw his wife and the blessed abode of the Spirits where all was plenty and all was joy, and he was glad.

---

[10] The animal characters all had human personalities and could talk in the mythical "ancient times," but their descendents are said to have lost these attributes. Powell used the Indian names for the characters in the myths; for example, "Ta-vwoats" or Rabbit. For clarity the English names have been substituted with an indication in brackets of the Indian name.

"Now when they had returned Rabbit enjoined upon the chief that he should never travel this trail again during life, and that all his people should be warned not to walk therein. Yet still he feared that they would attempt it so he rolled a river into trail—a mad raging river into the gorge made by the globe of fire, which should overwhelm any who might seek to enter there.

"The Origin of the Mountains, Valleys, [and] Cañons"

"Originally the surface of the Earth was a smooth plain, but one day Coyote [Shin-au-av] told Hawk [Kusav] to place the latter's quiver at a short distance from where they stood that it might be used as a mark, at which he would shoot. Then Coyote sent an arrow from his bow which struck the quiver, but glanced and plowed its way about the face of the earth in every conceivable direction, digging deep gorges and canons, making valleys, plowing up mountains, hills, and rocks. In this way the water courses were determined and the hills and mountains made and huge rocks were scattered about the country.

"Origin of the Pai-Utes"

"The Pai-Utes have a number of stories about an Old Woman of the Sea, many of which I have not been able to understand. One has been told me several times, and it is believed the substance has been obtained.

"Old Woman of the Sea [Si-chom-pa Ka-gon] came out of the sea with a sack filled with something and securely tied. Then she went to the home of the Shin-au-av brothers [Wolf and Coyote] carrying her burden with her, which was very heavy, and bent her nearly to the ground. When she found the brothers she delivered to them the sack and told them to carry it into the middle of the world and open it, and enjoined upon them that they should not look into it until their arrival at the designated point and there they would meet Rabbit [Ta-vwoats], who would tell them what to do with it. Then the Old Woman went back to the sea disappearing in the waters.

"Wolf gave the sack to Coyote and told him to do as the Old Woman had directed, and especially enjoined upon him that he must not open the sack lest some calamity should befall him. He found it very heavy and with great difficulty he carried it along by short stages and as he proceeded, his curiosity to know what it contained became greater and greater. 'Maybe,' said he, 'it is sand; maybe it is dung! who knows but what the old woman is playing a trick!' Many times he tried to feel the outside of the sack to discover what it contained. At one-time he thought it was full of snakes; at another, full of lizards. 'So,' said he, 'it is full of fishes.' At last his curiosity overcame him and he untied the sack, when out sprang hosts of people who passed out on the plain shouting and running toward the mountain. Coyote overcome with fright, threw himself down on the sand. Then Rabbit suddenly appeared and grasping the neck of the sack tied it up, being very angry with Coyote. 'Why,' said he, 'have you done this? I wanted these people to live in that good land to the east and here, foolish boy, you have let them out in a desert.'

"There were yet a few people left in the sack and Rabbit took it to the Kaibab Plateau to the brink of the Grand Canyon and there took out the remainder where the food was abundant on the cliffs, and herds of game wandered in the forests.

"These are the Pai-Utes, the true Utes, the others have scattered over the world and live in many places."

Powell collected other data on the Ute, Southern Paiute, and other Indians of the Canyon Country and the Great Basin. Much of it consists of vocabulary lists, lists of chiefs and headmen, myths and tales, and miscellaneous notes. It is lamentable that Powell never found time to complete his intended monograph on the "Numa." He clearly knew more than he wrote down, but the knowledge died with him.

Nevertheless, Powell called attention to the anthropology of the Canyon Country—the silent ruins of past cultures, as well as the historic tribes—and to the need for systematic study of these cultures and peoples. Others have heeded the call and taken up the work. The Canyon Country and adjacent areas are one of the best known areas of North America anthropologically. A large part of the accumulated anthropological data was gathered by employees of Powell's Bureau of American Ethnology, who continued the work begun by Powell. The knowledge gained by these persons, as well as by later workers from many other institutions, serves well as a fitting monument to Powell —the first anthropologist of the Canyon Country.

REFERENCES CITED

Aikens, C. M., 1966, Fremont-Promontory-Plains relationships; including a report of excavations at the Injun Creek and Bear River number 1 sites, northern Utah: Utah Univ., Dept. Anthropology, Anthropol. Papers, no. 82, 102 p.

REFERENCES CITED

Bartlett, R. A., 1962, Great surveys of the American West: Norman, Okla., Univ. Oklahoma Press, 408 p.

Bolton, Herbert, 1950, Pageant in the wilderness; the story of the Escalante Expedition to the Interior Basin, 1776: Utah Hist. Quart., v. 18, p. 1–265.

Cline, G. G., 1963, Exploring the Great Basin: Norman, Okla., Univ. Oklahoma Press, 254 p.

Creer, L. H., 1958, The activities of Jacob Hamblin in the region of the Colorado: Utah Univ., Dept. Anthropology, Anthropol. Papers, no. 33, 40 p.

Darrah, W. E., ed., 1947, Biographical sketches and original documents of the first Powell expedition of 1869: Utah Hist. Quart., v. 15, p. 1–148.

――― 1951, Powell of the Colorado: Princeton, N.J., Princeton Univ. Press, 426 p.

Darrah, W. C., Chamberlin, R. V., and Kelly, Charles, eds., 1947, Biographical sketches and original documents of the second Powell expedition of 1871–72: Utah Hist. Quart., v. 15, p. 149–270.

Darrah, W. C., Gregory, H. E., and Kelly, Charles, eds., 1948–49, The exploration of the Colorado River and the High Plateaus of Utah of the second Powell expedition of 1871–72: Utah Hist. Quart., v. 16–17, p. 1–540.

Dellenbaugh, F. S., 1908, A canyon voyage—The narrative of the second Powell expedition down the Green-Colorado River from Wyoming and the explorations on land, in the years 1871 and 1872: New York, G. P. Putnam's Sons, 277 p. (Also available in paperback, with a Foreword by W. H. Goetzmann: New Haven, Yale Univ. Press, 1962, 277 p.)

Dutton, C. E., 1880, Report on the geology of the High Plateaus of Utah: Washington, D.C., U.S. Geog. and Geol. Survey Rocky Mtn. Region (Powell), 307 p.

Euler, R. C., 1966a, Willow figurines from Arizona: Nat. History, v. 75, no. 3, p. 62–67.

――― 1966b, Southern Paiute ethnohistory: Utah Univ., Dept. Anthropology, Anthropol. Papers, no. 78, 173 p.

――― 1967, The canyon dwellers: Am. West, v. 4, no. 2, p. 22–27, 67–71.

Euler, R. C., and Olsen, A. P., 1965, Split twig figurines from northern Arizona—New radiocarbon dates: Science, v. 148, no. 3668, p. 368–369.

Euler, R. C., and Taylor, W. W., 1966, Additional archaeological data from upper Grand Canyon—Nankoweap to Unkar revisited: Plateau, v. 39, no. 1, p. 26–45.

Fowler, D. D., and Fowler, C. S., 1969a, John Wesley Powell's journal of his second Colorado River expedition, 1871–72: Smithsonian Jour. History, v. 3, no. 3. (In press.)

――― 1969b, The anthropology of the Numa—John Wesley Powell's manuscripts on the Indians of the Desert West: Smithsonian Contr. Anthropology. (In press.)

Gilbert, G. K., 1877, Report on the geology of the Henry Mountains: Washington, D.C., U.S. Geog. and Geol. Survey Rocky Mtn. Region (Powell), 160 p.

Goetzmann, W. H., 1959, Army exploration in the American West, 1803–1863: New Haven, Yale Univ. Press, 509 p.

Goss, J. A., 1968, Culture-historical inference from Utaztekan linguistic evidence, in Swanson, E. H., Jr., ed., Utaztekan prehistory: Idaho State Univ. Mus. Occas. Papers, no. 22, p. 1–42.

Gregory, H. E., ed., 1939, Diary of Almon Harris Thompson: Utah Hist. Quart., v. 7, p. 1–140.

Haines, Francis, 1938, The northward spread of horses among the Plains Indians: Am. Anthropologist, v. 40, p. 429–437.

Hall, E. T., 1942, Archaeological survey of Walhalla Glades: Mus. Northern Arizona Bull. 20, 32 p.

Haury, E. W., 1932, Kivas of the Tusayan Ruin, Grand Canyon, Arizona: Gila Pueblo Medallion Papers, no. 9, 26 p.

James, G. W., 1900, In and around the Grand Canyon; the Grand Canyon of the Colorado River in Arizona: Boston, Little Brown and Co., 341 p.

Jennings, J. D., 1964, The Desert West, in Jennings, J. D., and Norbeck, E., eds., Prehistoric man in the New World: Chicago, Univ. Chicago Press, p. 149–175.

――― 1965, Later specializations, in Spencer, R. F., and Jennings, J. D., eds., The native Americans: New York, Harper and Row, p. 57–99.

――― 1966, Glen Canyon—A summary: Utah Univ., Dept. Anthropology, Anthropol. Papers, no. 81, 84 p.

Judd, N. H., 1926, Archeological observations north of the Rio Colorado: U. S. Bur. Am. Ethnology Bull. 82, 171 p.

Lipe, W. D., 1960, 1958 excavations, Glen Canyon area: Utah Univ., Dept. Anthropology, Anthropol. Papers, no. 44, 241 p.

McNutt, C. H., and Euler, R. C., 1966, The Red Butte lithic sites near Grand Canyon, Arizona: Am. Antiquity, v. 31, p. 410–419.

Miller, W. R., 1966, Anthropological linguistics in the Great Basin, in Great Basin Anthropological Conference, 9th, University of Nevada, 1964, The current status of anthropological research in the Great Basin, 1964. Edited by W. L. d'Azevedo and others: Nevada Univ., Desert Research Inst., Tech. Rept. Ser.: Social Sci. and Humanities Pubs., no. 1, p. 75–112.

Powell, J. W., 1874, Report of explorations in 1873 of the Colorado River of the West and its tributaries: Washington, D.C., U.S. Govt. Printing Office, 36 p.

――― 1875a, Exploration of the Colorado River of the West and its tributaries: Washington, D.C., U.S. Govt. Printing Office, 291 p.

――― 1875b, The ancient province of Tusayan: Scribner's Monthly, v. 11, p. 193–213.

――― 1875c, An overland trip to the Grand Cañon: Scribner's Monthly, v. 10, p. 659–678.

――― 1876, Report on the geology of the eastern portion of the Uinta Mountains and a region of country adjacent thereto: Washington, D.C., U.S. Geol. and Geog. Survey Terr. (Powell), 218 p.

――― 1895, Canyons of the Colorado: Meadville, Pa., Flood and Vincent, 400 p. (Also available in paperback under title: The exploration of the Colorado River and its canyons: New York, Dover Pubs., 1961, 400 p.)

Powell, J. W., and Ingalls, G. W., 1874, Report of special commissioners J. W. Powell and G. W. Ingalls on the conditions of the Ute Indians of Utah; the Pai-Utes of Utah, northern Arizona, southern Nevada, and southeastern California; the Go-Si-Utes of Utah and Nevada; the northwestern Shoshones of Idaho and Utah; and the western Shoshones of Nevada; and report concerning claims of settlers in the Mo-a-pa Valley (southeastern Nevada): Washington, D.C., U.S. Govt. Printing Office, 36 p.

Schwartz, D. W., 1960, Archaeological investigations in the Shinumo area of Grand Canyon, Arizona: Plateau, v. 32, no. 3, p. 61–67.

———— 1963, An archaeological survey of Nankoweap Canyon, Grand Canyon National Park: Am. Antiquity, v. 28, p. 289–302.

———— 1965, Nankoweap to Unkar—An archaeological survey of the upper Grand Canyon: Am. Antiquity, v. 30, p. 278–296.

Shimkin, D. B., 1940, Shoshoni-Comanche origins and migrations: Pacific Sci. Cong., 6th, Berkeley, Calif., 1939, Proc., v. 4, p. 17–25.

Stanton, R. C., 1965, Down the Colorado. Edited, with an introduction, by D. L. Smith: Norman, Okla., Univ. Oklahoma Press, 237 p.

Stegner, Wallace, 1954, Beyond the Hundredth Meridian—John Wesley Powell and the second opening of the American West: Boston, Houghton Mifflin, 438 p. (Also available in paperback: Sentry Edition, Boston, Houghton Mifflin, 1962, 438 p.)

Steward, J. H., 1938, Basin-Plateau aboriginal sociopolitical groups: U. S. Bur. Am. Ethnology Bull. 120, 346 p.

———— 1939, Notes on Hillers' photographs of the Paiute and Ute Indians taken on the Powell expedition of 1873: Smithsonian Misc. Collns., v. 98, no. 18, 23 p.

Stewart, O. C., 1958, Shoshone history and social organization: Congreso Internac. Americanistas, 33d, San Jose, Costa Rica, 1958, Actas, p. 134–142.

Taylor, W. W., 1958, Two archaeological studies in northern Arizona; the Pueblo ecology study: haii and farewell, and a brief survey through the Grand Canyon of the Colorado River: Mus. Northern Arizona Bull. 30, 30 p.

Weller, Ted, 1959, San Juan Triangle Survey, in Fowler, D. D., and others, The Glen Canyon Archeological Survey, Part II: Utah Univ., Dept. Anthropology, Anthropol. Papers, no. 39, p. 319–707.

Wilder, C. S., 1944, Archaeological survey of the Great Thumb area, Grand Canyon National Park: Plateau, v. 17, no. 2, p. 17–26.

Wormington, H. M., 1956, Prehistoric Indians of the Southwest: 3d ed., Denver, Colo., Denver Mus. Nat. History, 191 p.